THEN AND THERE SERIES
GENERAL EDITOR
MARJORIE REEVES, M.A., PH.D.

Parliamentary
Elections and Reform
(1807-1832)

JOHN ADDY, M.A., D.R.E. (LEEDS)

Illustrated from contemporary sources by

BARBOSA

LONGMAN

LONGMAN GROUP LIMITED
London

Associated companies, branches and representatives
throughout the world

First published 1961
Eighth impression 1977

ISBN 0 582 20379 1

ACKNOWLEDGMENTS

We are grateful to the following for permission to quote copyright material:

Dr G. R. Batho for material from a teaching unit on the election; the Earl Fitzwilliam for extracts from the Lord Milton material; the Earl of Harewood for extracts from the Lascelles material; Lord Halifax for the use of election posters; Mrs Spencer Stanhope for extracts from tne Stanhope correspondence; Mr W. E. Tate for an unpublished article on the election of 1807.

The maps on pages 54 and 73 are drawn from Gayler, Richards and Morris: *A Sketch-Map History of Britain* and *A Sketch-Map Economic History of Britain* respectively, by permission of George G. Harrap & Co, Ltd.

Printed in Hong Kong by
Dai Nippon Printing Co., (H.K.) Ltd.

CONTENTS

TO THE READER

The various Reform Acts between 1832 and 1887 swept
away the whole of the old election procedure and customs
and this book attempts to recapture the hectic conditions
under which elections were conducted in England before
1832. It also examines how the movement for reform
gradually developed.

All the extracts in this book are taken from the original
sources and much of this material has never been used
since the day that it was first published for use at the
election. Every picture in this book was originally drawn
by some artist who was alive during the eighteenth and
early nineteenth centuries. As you read the book, it is
hoped that you will recognize the individuals who appear
in its pages as those who actually made the speeches and
published the various pamphlets and ballads. They will
become real people, as indeed they were.

At the end of the book you will find a list of Things to
Do and this has been planned to encourage you to find
out for yourselves more about the history of elections that
took place before and after 1832 in your own district.

The Yorkshire Election 1807

Do you go to a school which is used as a *Polling Station* when we elect M.P.s? If so, you will know that on election day the school children have a holiday. Outside the school, policemen stand on duty and no one is allowed in unless his name is on the *Register of Voters*. Inside the school little cubby-holes have been made with wooden screens round them so that no one can see how you vote. Everyone behaves in a most solemn and orderly way. Each voter's name is checked, then he takes his voting paper to one of the voting places and when he has made his vote he drops the paper through a slot in a big box called the *Ballot Box*, which is specially sealed so that no one can open it until the right time.

The rules are very strict and there is a man in charge, called the *Returning Officer*, who makes everyone keep them. You must vote between 8 a.m. and 9 p.m. on the same day. If you make a disturbance or try to make someone else vote the way you want or even try to see how they vote, you may be disqualified, that is, not allowed to vote yourself. The vote or *ballot* is secret. No one dares to break the seals and open the boxes until the right time. After 9 p.m. all the boxes from all the polling stations are taken to the Town Hall, or County Hall, or Urban District Council Offices and there the votes are counted with lots of people watching to see that no one cheats.

All these rules have been made so that elections shall be

as fair as possible. Only the people with a right to vote must do so and they must be free to vote exactly as they like, without being afraid of anyone. No one must *bribe* the voters, that is, give them money for their votes. *Candidates* cannot spend more than a certain sum on the election. So we try to stop *bribery* in elections, that is buying and selling votes. We want all voters to be 'free'—to vote simply for the candidates they think the best.

But in 1807 elections were by no means as free as this. In those days the M.P.s were usually rich men, noble landowners, country gentlemen, merchants or bankers. They did not spend much time going around making speeches to persuade people to vote for them. More often they bribed or frightened the voters into voting for them. Half the time there was not even an election; the same candidate or his son was *nominated* each time and, since no one dared to put up his name against the old family, the candidate got in unopposed.

There were then two kinds of election, as there are today—a borough election and a county one. In the borough it was fairly easy to make sure of the vote for there were not usually many electors to bribe. Two such examples are the Cornish boroughs of Camelford, with nine electors, and Saint Michael's with eighteen. At Gatton in Surrey there was one elector. In the counties, everyone with *freehold* land worth 40/- or more had the vote, so there might be thousands of voters, as in Yorkshire, or only six hundred as in Rutland. If the candidate had to bribe all these it was very expensive. What the great noble families liked to do was to get a whole county into their power so that they could fix the election just as they wished. There were two M.P.s for each county, so it would be arranged that the most important family would choose one member or control one seat, as we say, and the best known country gentleman would take the other seat.

This was allright if all the chief families could agree, but counties often had several of these, each of whom thought that it was the chief family. When these families failed to reach an agreement there was a disputed election with several candidates. There was nothing orderly about this; it was one grand fight in which the candidates spilled money all round the county, kept the free beer flowing and even egged on their supporters to knock a few people down and break their heads. It was an exciting time. This was the kind of election which took place in Yorkshire in 1807. There had not been a disputed election there for sixty years and I expect the people looked forward to a bit of excitement: they got it! The leading Yorkshire family at this time was headed by the second Earl Fitzwilliam who owned 22,000 acres of land in Yorkshire alone. He also had large estates in Northampton and Huntingdon. These estates, as well as the big family estates in Ireland, brought the Earl an income which amounted to over £150,000 every year. It will not surprise you to find that Earl Fitzwilliam claimed that it was his right to nominate one of the Yorkshire members himself and so he put forward his son, Lord Milton, who was not yet twenty-one years of age. Lord Milton was already an M.P. for Malton, the Yorkshire borough in which his father owned the greater part of the property. Where a single family owned sufficient property in a borough to influence the election, the borough became known as a *Pocket Borough* and it was no uncommon thing for these to be bought and sold like expensive pieces of merchandise. The other member was William Wilberforce, who was a Yorkshireman and he had recently guided the Bill to abolish the Slave Trade through the House of Commons. You will remember that Wilberforce had worked very hard to help the slaves and sometimes people spoke of this in the election. Wilberforce had represented the county since 1784 and his chief supporters were the country squires of the East Riding.

By 1807 a rival family had come to the fore both in wealth and influence and was resolved to challenge the supremacy of the Fitzwilliams. This was the family of Lascelles who lived at Harewood House near Leeds. They were not yet so rich or so powerful as the Fitzwilliams but they owned 20,000 acres of land in Yorkshire as well as large sugar *plantations* in the island of Barbados. The family fortune had been founded by the first earl who acted as collector of Customs in Barbados. Both families probably felt that their reputation was in danger and either stood to win or lose through the election, so that both families spent their money like water in an attempt to win the election.

The Election Campaign

The Election was to be held on May 7th 1807. You are all familiar with the colours that are worn by the candidates who represent the various parties in the elections of today. The Liberals wear yellow colours, the Conservatives blue and the Labour candidates red. In 1807 there was no custom like this. Wilberforce wore pink, Lascelles selected blue and Lord Milton decided to wear orange as his colour. The contest began when the Sheriff of Yorkshire summoned a meeting at York Castle for the

York Castle—the County's headquarters

purpose of nominating the candidates. If you look at the illustration you will see the place where the Sheriff used to hold the meeting and this was the site where the election *hustings* were put up. You will remember that there had been no contested election in Yorkshire for sixty years and the Sheriff was hoping to avoid such an election this time, for elections often led to fighting and rioting between the supporters of various candidates.

The only people who were supposed to attend the nomination meeting were those who had the right to vote in the election, but when the meeting was announced large numbers of people turned up on the day, whether they had a vote or not, just to look at the candidates and take part in the nomination proceedings. At any rate it was an excuse for a short holiday outing for many. The Sheriff opened the meeting and called for nominations; all the time he was secretly hoping that there would be only two nominations so that he could avoid the trouble of a contested election. However, to his dismay, three candidates were nominated, Wilberforce, Lascelles and Lord Milton, and were all duly seconded for the two county seats. All this was done by *show of hands* and then counting, or attempting to count correctly, the number of the raised hands in favour of each candidate. The Sheriff was quite prepared to make a decision that the majority were in favour of Wilberforce and Lascelles. Unfortunately for the Sheriff, Lord Milton's father, the Earl Fitzwilliam, raised an objection so that an election was necessary. Earl Fitzwilliam said afterwards that 'Mr Lascelles had made sure of a contest by packing the nomination meeting with all his friends whether they had the right to vote or not'.

When Mr Lascelles heard of this remark he had a hand-

6

bill printed which he circulated around the county attacking those who wished to avoid an election. The handbill read like this.

Friends and Supporters of
MR LASCELLES
Conceiving that the
SHEW OF HANDS
At the nomination meeting held
this day was decidely in favour
and
THE SHERIFF
having declared
THE FACT TO BE SO
call upon the Freeholders in general
to support what so clearly seems
to be
THE SENSE OF THE COUNTY
and to use their utmost exertions for
the purpose of preserving
THE PEACE OF THE COUNTY
against those who appear inclined
further to disturb it by
REFUSING TO ABIDE BY THE DECISION
OF THIS DAY

When Earl Fitzwilliam read this he was very cross and if you read the handbill very carefully you will discover why. So he had a letter printed which was addressed to the electors of Yorkshire. One of Earl Fitzwilliam's supporters had been at a meeting addressed by Mr Lascelles in which the speaker had said that 'he was sick of the whole business'. It was this remark which gave him the idea of the letter which follows. Now read this very carefully.

THE SICK CANDIDATE TO THE
FREEHOLDERS
OF THE COUNTY OF YORK

Gentlemen:

Mr Lascelles has told you that the Sense of the County was clearly expressed at the Day of Nomination and was decidedly in his favour. The former part of this Assertion is unfounded. The Sense of the Freeholders of this great County was not expressed at that meeting for Nineteen out of Twenty were not present and not One in Four of those present were Voters.

LORD MILTON having determined upon a Poll considered a large shew of hands on this Occasion as unimportant and did not press the attendance of many of his friends. But on the part of Mr Lascelles uncommon Pains were taken to insure a numerous Attendance and the Populace of York, naturally interested in obtaining a Poll being told by his confidential Friends that Mr Lascelles was half sick of the Business already, crowded in shoals to the Castle Yard anxious to cheer the drooping spirits of Mr Lascelles and to urge him on to the Contest.

LORD MILTON

Can you see why the people of York were anxious to have an election? An election would bring much trade to the city in providing food and drink and lodging accommodation for the voters, the candidates and their supporters. They also knew that money would be spent like water and that the citizens would be able to make a handsome profit out of a contested election. So you will not be surprised to learn that the people of York did all they could to make the contest a keen one.

There were two Yorkshire newspapers which the rival candidates could rely upon for support and to stir up the excitement. The *Leeds Mercury* which had become a Whig paper in 1801 of course supported the Fitzwilliams. The *Leeds Intelligencer* as a Tory paper was wholeheartedly in favour of Lascelles. The candidates themselves wanted to conduct the election in the traditional

8

style, which meant that certain arrangements were made between the candidates about the conduct of the election, but their supporters refused to recognize these and resolved to put all their energies into the contest and have a real fight. So you will understand that the election *pamphlets* which were put out by both sides were often very rude and pointed in their remarks.

Of course each candidate looked round for some way of attacking his rival. Lord Lascelles began by printing a pamphlet which he circulated all round Yorkshire attacking Lord Milton. Young Fitzwilliam, Lord Milton, was only a fortnight past his twenty-first birthday when the election began and he had held the family pocket borough of Malton in the previous parliament. He was young, enthusiastic, pale, slender, and very boyish in his appearance; he had married at the age of twenty. As the Tories were quick to point out, he was a very young man indeed. Although he was a member of the Church of England, he was in favour of granting freedom of worship to Roman Catholics, who had not been allowed this privilege since 1559 and also to Protestant Dissenters who had been under penalties for not attending the services of the Church of England since 1662. Using all these points, Lascelles put out the following poster.

WANTED
A YOUNG WOMAN
accustomed to the care of
CHILDREN
To superintend a
GROWN BABY.
APPLY AT W—— TW——H HOUSE
If IRISH and a ROMAN CATHOLIC she
will be preferred.

Can you see how cleverly the attack on Lord Milton is disguised? He is the 'grown baby' and the reference to the Irish and Roman Catholics is to his father who was Lord Lieutenant of Ireland for a time. Both were in favour of *toleration* for Catholics. You will notice that certain letters have been missed out of the name of Lord Milton's house. If this had been printed in full it could have ended in a charge of *libel*. The *Leeds Intelligencer* followed this poster by publishing two poems or songs which supported this. Here is a short extract from the first. It is entitled 'TO QUIET A BABY', and is intended to be sung to the tune of 'Paddy Whack'.

> To quiet a baby that cried for the County
>   The old women of Yorkshire were called in to try,
> Whoever would attend him was offer'd a bounty,
>   His Irish wet nurses were lately run dry.
> At Malton his rattle was stole by the Freemen
>   The go-cart at York slipt from under his feet
> So they came in a body, and all the old women,
>   Are hushing the baby and wiping him sweet.

And Tim Trimmer wrote a verse which was supposed to have been sung by 'the wet nurse, lately hired by Lord F—z——m for the infant Candidate'

> Poor little Fitz
> Has lost his wits
> And can't tell where to find them;
> Let him alone
> Till F——w——s comes home,
> And brings his votes behind him.

The reference here is to Lord Milton's agent, Mr Fawkes of Farnley Hall, Leeds.

The Whigs were not slow to make a counter-attack.

Lord Lascelles was a nervous and rather weak speaker who frequently lost his temper. He did so at one of his election meetings in Leeds and foolishly described the Yorkshire voters as 'a parcel of disaffected ragamuffins', and so his opponents put out the following poster;

WANTED
A Hundred
NEGRO DRIVERS
To be employed in the
ISLAND OF
BARBADOS
Apply at H——w——d House
No Yorkshire Clothier need apply as they have been found too refractory to be insulted and trampled upon by
THE SON OF THE PROPRIETOR.
Should the Slave Trade be revived in the next session of Parliament with a view to which the Proprietor is labouring to procure for his Son the Representation of the COUNTY of YORK, the number of NEGRO DRIVERS will not be limited but may extend to TWO THOUSAND at least.

Now have you spotted that this pamphlet was against Lord Lascelles? Parliament had abolished the slave trade only a little while before the election, and Lord Milton was quick to see that he could work up the sympathies of everyone who was against slavery to support his own cause. You will remember that Lord Lascelles' family had made its fortune in sugar plantations in the Barbados. This meant the use of slave labour and so Lord Milton was able to use the argument: 'If you let Lascelles into Parliament he will bring back the slave trade.'

Another Whig attack suggested that after Mr Lascelles' election, when he has ruined the Yorkshire cloth trade, he would no longer be able to obtain negroes from Africa to serve on his father's West Indies plantations. Then doubtless he would export, as slaves, shiploads of West Riding clothiers from the Huddersfield and Leeds cloth halls. Several newspaper articles suggested that because Lascelles had interests in the sugar plantations of the Barbados he would have an interest in the revival of the 'bloody slave traffic', and therefore every man who gave him a vote would be 'stained with the blood of Africans'. Again it was said, 'the gold which will convey Mr Lascelles' voters to the poll has been drawn from the injured natives of Africa.' The *Leeds Mercury* supported this poster with a poem entitled, 'The Clothiers Friend'. Here is an extract.

> Ye Yorkshire Clothiers all attend,
>   And join in hand and heart, Sirs,
> Come vote for the man, Who'll be your friend
>   And each good purpose answers.
>
> L——d H——e——d's paw fain would you awe,
>   And hold you in submission;
> But let them see you dare be free,
>   And have them in derision.
>
> Make haste and poll, fill the roll
>   With honest votes for Milton
> Pack off the knaves with negro slaves
>   And send them all to *Plumpton*.
>
> Each take a cup of good stout ale,
>   And relish it with Stilton
> No slavery here, no treacle beer,
>   Let's drink success to Milton.
>   MILTON FOR EVER—NO TREACLE BEER.

Plumpton was a pocket borough which had been pur-chased from the profits of the sugar plantations. It was reported that the staple drink for the enslaved Yorkshire clothiers in the Barbados would be beer made from treacle, the latter, as you know, being a product of the sugar-cane.

Of course the supporters of Lord Milton did not have the battle all their own way. In reply to the charges made against Mr Lascelles, his supporters put out a series of questions and answers in a pamphlet entitled:

NO MILTON
NO POPERY

QUERIES	ANSWERS
1 What Lord Lieutenant of Ireland was recalled by his Sovereign after three months of his administration?	THE FATHER OF LORD MILTON
2 Who removed from Office in Ireland all the friends of Mr Pitt?	THE FATHER OF LORD MILTON
3 Who brought forward a bill to make popery the established religion of Ireland?	THE FATHER OF LORD MILTON
4 Who has favoured and justified the disaffected Irish?	THE FATHER OF LORD MILTON

Therefore—NO MILTON—NO POPERY

Can you see how the opponents of Lord Milton pick out the weak points of Earl Fitzwilliam's career as Lord Lieutenant of Ireland and try to use them to the advantage of Mr Lascelles? It was still easy to arouse opposition to Roman Catholics, for Englishmen had a fear of Rome and the Pope that dated from the events of the reign of James II.

In Leeds, as elsewhere, excitement developed as soon as the nominations were made. On Tuesday, May 19th,

13

the Mayor of Leeds, Richard Bramley who was a Tory, was watching a procession through the city in favour of Mr Lascelles when a small boy offended him by shouting, 'Milton for ever'. The Mayor seized the small boy and soundly boxed his ears. The citizens rescued the lad and so hustled the Mayor that he read the Riot Act and instead of calling the local constables to restore order, he called out a troop of Inniskilling Dragoons. They galloped through the streets and even entered private houses to arrest or silence suspected Whigs. The *Leeds Intelligencer* came out with the following comments.

> Ye friends of order, use your eyes,
> See what a mighty difference lies
> 'Twixt Dickey Bramley, road surveyor
> And Richard Ramsden Bramley, Mayor;
> The point is clear—they're different beats,
> This *scours* the ditches—that the streets.

This seems to have been followed by a threat to break the windows of the Mayor's house, and since the Prince of Wales had offered the sum of five guineas for the detection of the persons who had broken his windows at Brighton, the *Intelligencer* printed this:

> COMPAR'D with Princes, what a mind
> In B——y Mayor of Leeds we find;
> When royal panes were broke, we heard
> Five guineas was the small reward;
> But for his worship's panes we see
> One hundred guineas is the fee.

And an equally sharp comment upon the Mayor's action in calling out the troops at election time.

To Mr B——y, Mayor of Leeds, and his Iniskillen Dragoons.

> Tis surely unfair
> In a Protestant Mayor,
> And his party must feel very sore,
> That he who rail's most
> At the Pope and his host,
> Should call out a Catholic corps.

For the Dragoons were an Irish regiment and the Mayor was a very strong Protestant.

If you will look at the illustration below you will notice how the candidates and their supporters *canvassed*

The agents of the rival candidates asking for votes

15

for votes. Have you noticed that while the agent is asking the people outside the inn to vote for him, a party is attacking the inn lower down the street and taking down the sign? This was the centre of the rival candidate. We know something of the canvassing that took place in Yorkshire when we read a letter written by an estate agent to his master, Mr Spencer Stanhope of Cawthorne, near Barnsley. As you read this you will be able to discover how the supporters of each candidate worked amongst the voters.

Tivy Dale
May 7th 1807.

Mr Stanhope,
I hope your bustle is nearly over and that you have so far got it thro' to your satisfaction. The County here is now busy indeed. I have been at Penistone today as were several others Canvassing—say two from Sheffield for Mr Lascelles—The Revd Mr Corbet from Wortley for the same and Lord Milton. Jackson was also there for Lord Milton.
I am told that Colonel Beaumont and Mr Wentworth's interests are both for Mr Lascelles and Lord Milton.

JOHN HOWSON

As well as issuing pamphlets, many election *ballads* were composed and sung throughout the whole country and some of these were very rude indeed to the various candidates. Here are three verses from a ballad which was sung at York and made fun of Lord Milton.

(Tune—'Vicar and Moses')

'What a Lordling it is
With his carrotty phiz,
So wide eyed, so flattered, so built on,
One may oft take a Rule
From a nickname at School,
And the boys called him Old Lady Milton.

O Patriot revered,
Go, shave for a beard,
Hi to Wentworth and finish this strife.
York, Malton, the County,
Disdain to be bound to ye,
Go live with your nice little wife.

O soon may she bear,
You a fine son and heir
Then ten oxen whole you may roast.
May Fitzwilliam carouse
With TWO boys in the House
Nor bewail Milton's *Paradise Lost*.'

The reference to the roasting of ten oxen is to a banquet which was given at the family seat at Wentworth Woodhouse for 10,000 electors, all the food and drink being free of charge. It was expected that Lord Milton would lose the election and so there is the reference to the poem by John Milton which is entitled *Paradise Lost*. John Milton lived about 150 years before this time.

Canvassing for votes took place each day and those who lived in or were familiar with a particular district would undertake to canvass it. They set out with the private cards of the candidates fixed to long wands, and a band accompanied the canvassers to excite people by music. For generations there had been two bands in York which played music for the elections. One was the *Blue Band* led by the families of Hardman and Bean, while the other was the *Orange Band* led by Mr Walker's family. To keep excitement alive, night canvassing took place accompanied by a band known as a lighted tar-band, because the players were accompanied by people carrying torches made of hemp soaked in tar. These were excuses for frequent calls at public houses on the pretence that much refreshment was necessary. If a good crowd collected then a thirty-six-gallon barrel of beer was rolled into the street and set up on end. When the butt end had been opened all were invited to help themselves, which they did, drinking out of all kinds of utensils (even hats) and wasting much beer in the process. And so the grand day got nearer and nearer when the poll was to be opened at York.

Buying votes with money

The Poll

In a modern election, as I said at the beginning, the poll opens and closes on the same day, with the voters going to register their vote in one of the local schools. In 1807 there was no such arrangement. Each candidate had to arrange for the transport of his supporters to York and the poll was open for fifteen days. Instructions giving information about the arrangements that had been made for transporting the voters to York were issued by the candidates. Here is a copy of Lord Milton's notice.

TO THE FREEHOLDERS OF YORKSHIRE
Those GENTLEMEN who have so handsomely come forward
to support
LORD MILTON
At the ensuing ELECTION for the Representatives of
the COUNTY OF YORK:
Are respectfully informed of the arrangements that are made for their CONVEYANCE TO THE POLL and the several Carriages and other Accommodation for their CONVENIENCE are already provided. (And the dival will bring back.)
LORD MILTON'S COMMITTEE will take Care to *apprize* in due time the GENTLEMEN FREEHOLDERS in his Interest, of the respective places where the Carriages and other Conveyances are stationed that as little Delay or Inconvenience may arise as possible.
York, May 17th 1807.

Have you noticed that some opponent of Lord Milton has tried to deface this notice by writing across it the words

Voters travelling to York by fast coach

'And the dival will bring back.' (Dival is a word you
know quite well only wrongly spelt. I leave you to spot
what it is.) The leaflet was trying to persuade the voters
that they would be able to make the long journey to York
and back again to their homes very quickly and com-
fortably. All the voters were to be brought by road or
water to York. Barges were hired to convey the voters of

Travelling in a phaeton to York

Leeds along the river Aire and those from Hull were brought up the river Ouse. For those who came from the remote parts of the county and from places outside, such as London, Manchester and Sheffield, accommodation had to be booked at hotels along the route, and the voters who had to spend one or more nights were lodged at the candidate's expense.

Lord Milton booked thirty inns for his supporters at such places as Easingwold, Thirsk and Tadcaster. He also reserved over one hundred houses in York at which his supporters could sleep. How costly all this was you can see for yourself as you read that Lord Milton's bill for his supporters at the *Rose and Crown* in York, for 112 persons was £157 12s. and his bill at the *Red Lion* was

A wagon load for York

more than £1,300. Many voters remained in York for the whole fifteen days enjoying themselves at the candidates expense and one party ran up a bill of £2,630 which Mr Lascelles had to pay. Even the cost of transport was no small item for Lord Milton. His charge for conveying the 221 voters of West Gilling to York and back, a distance of twenty miles, was £1,900. It is not surprising that the aldermen of Leeds opened a subscription fund to assist Mr Lascelles with his expenses.

The whole county was now boiling with excitement over the election. Party spirit was whipped up by the friends of the two noble families and everything that money, or influence, or personal energy could do to bring success was carried out. Dozens of people must have got drunk on the free beer; at the *Cross Keys*, in York, no less than sixty gallons of free beer were drunk—paid for by Mr Lascelles. Wilberforce and Lascelles encouraged their supporters by this song.

> On Wednesday next the twentieth May
> Is fixt for the Election
> Freemen and good will rue the day,
> If there should be defection,
> In voting 'gainst this Baby Lord,
> Who spite of all his boasting,
> Can hardly think that his bare word,
> Will save his ribs aroasting.
>
> Behold what loads are brought in carts
> All pack'd and screwd together,
> No doubt they'll nobly play their parts
> In spite of wind and weather.
> They'll lie and swear their votes are good
> Tho' scarcely one in twenty,
> Can state where'er his freehold stood
> Of such Lord Milton's plenty.

Wealthy voters used a private coach

As the poll got into its stride, the roads of the county were covered night and day with coaches, *barouches*, *curricles*, *gigs*, *fly wagons* and military carts, drawn by six or eight horses travelling at four miles an hour, all carrying the voters to York. As you look at the illustrations of the different methods of transport that were used, I wonder if you can name the people who would be likely to use each of these methods of transport? Earl

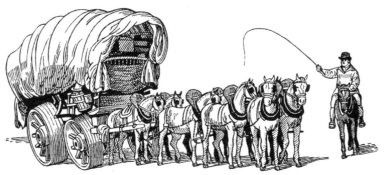

Even military carts like this were used to transport voters

23

A crowded coach prepares to leave for York

Fitzwilliam even brought bargeloads of voters from Hatfield to make sure that Lord Milton would get a majority. Going to an election was as much of a spree for our early nineteenth-century ancestors as a holiday on the continent is for us today. So everyone rolled in to York. The city was packed with voters. Every inn was engaged by one or the other candidate and unlimited quantities of food and drink were laid on for the entertainment of the voters. No expense was spared at this point and bands were hired to parade the streets singing and playing election songs like these

See the brave HARRY LASCELLES comes forth e'er the same,
Loyal zeal fires each breast at the sound of his name;
See, see, here he comes—with heart loyal and free,
Then to meet and support him each voter agree.
We will hail and we'll cheer him, again and again,
For he's proved himself steady,
Firm, loyal and ready,
To support King and Country again and again.

Here is one to encourage the supporters of Lord Milton.

COME cheer up my Lads—'tis by honour we steer,
Make haste to the poll—for Lord Milton appear:
For Milton, for Freedom, for Glory, for Fame;
For Milton the patriot no courtier you came:
Heart of Worth is our Lord, from our hearts are our Votes.
        We'll ever be ready,
        Steady, Boys, steady,
To Vote for our Milton—and ne'er turn our Coats.

Can you spot the well known tune to which these songs were intended to be sung?

The poll took place in the Castle Yard at York where fifteen *polling booths* were set up, one for each *wapentake*, arranged in the order shown in the illustration, so that each voter would know where to register his vote. Every elector when he arrived would go to the avenue which led to his polling booth and there he voted in public. Before he could do this he had to prove that he owned a freehold

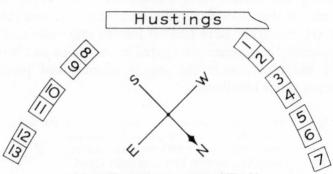

The polling booths were arranged like this

which was worth 40*s*. This might be a garden, or a house, or the *tithes* of a parish, or lands in a township. He had to describe his freehold and its situation with great care, and also name the *tenant* if there should be one renting a house or land of the freehold. The *Sheriff* then checked the claim to possess a vote by referring to the register of persons who paid *land tax* and finally the Sheriff's *assessors*, Samuel Heywood and John Bayley gave their decisions on the matter. Each candidate was allowed to have a *check clerk* at each of the booths and an agent to object to doubtful voters, for some persons who had no claim to vote often tried to do so. Mr Stanhope of Cawthorne, near Barnsley, acted as the check clerk for Mr Lascelles. These objections were written down, so that we can still read them. Here is one of them: you will notice that John and Christopher Alderson were objected to because they could not prove their title to the ownership of a freehold.

ATTESTATIONS TO VOTE
William Alderson is the Owner of an Estate at Birkdale in the Township of Reeth which he lets to his two sons John Alderson and

Christopher Alderson who are rated in the Land Tax as Owners. They occupy no other property under any other Persons and William Alderson will swear the whole they occupy is his.

Objected to by Lord Milton as not properly rated.

Not rated as occupiers.   T. PAUL

Rejected by John Bayley.

Altogether the Sheriff rejected 2,064 claims to a right to vote.

When a voter had proved his claim to be a freeholder the Sheriff gave him a certificate which read like this:

Thomas Appleby of Renishaw (Derby) Ironfounder has taken the Freeholder's oath prescribed by the 18th George the 2nd C.18 and has sworn that his freehold consists of House and Land in the Occupation of Phyllis Appleby lying and being at Barmingham in the County of York, before me this fourth day of June 1807.

SAMUEL GREEN

The person in possession of this, having taken the oath of a freeholder, had a right to vote. With this certificate in his hand, he then mounted the steps of the hustings and went to the right polling booth. Here he went through the entrance A, through the door B and publicly announced

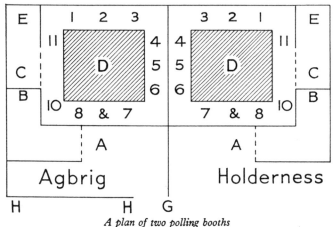

A plan of two polling booths

the name of the candidate he was voting for, in front of
the table, D, and then went out through the exit E. If
you look at the illustration you will see that all kinds of
persons were brought to the poll, even those who were
blind or crippled or feeble in mind, as the man in the
picture appears to be. Can you see the person who is
whispering in his ear the name of the candidate for whom

Both the lame and the mad went to vote

he is to vote? When a man had voted the poll clerk gave
him a certificate of his vote which enabled him to claim
expenses for his trip to York to vote. You see, a vote at
this time was regarded as a valuable piece of property
which was worth its price in money or in kind. Here is a

28

copy of a certificate which the vote had to produce when he claimed his expenses.

Wapentake of   William Appleton of Danby Wiske voted for Lord
East Gilling   Milton on the 11th days Poll.

THOMAS DANIEL
Poll Clerk for Lord Milton

On May 20th the poll was opened and remained open for so long as there were voters coming in. The state of the poll was declared each day and notes about its progress were sent out to all the parishes and townships in Yorkshire. Here is a copy of the one which was sent to Saddleworth in the heart of the Pennines on the road from Huddersfield to Manchester.

TO THE GENTLEMEN
FREEHOLDERS
AND
CLOTHIERS
OF
SADDLEWORTH.

It is to your assistance, exertions, and friendly support that I have all along looked and now more particularly rely upon, for bringing the present Contest to a Conclusion.

GENTLEMEN, I hope that, in your Opinion, I have done my part with Firmness and Decision; and I know you too well, and estimate your honest Endeavours, in my behalf, too highly, to hold any other Sentiment than Gratitude for the Countenance you have given me, and the highest confidence in your Support, for what yet remains to be accomplished.

For your Information, I give you the State of the Poll on Thursday; you will see from that, that Mr Lascelles is Two Hundred and Eighty-three a Head of Me—The poll is drawing to a very serious, decisive and interesting Crisis—It is to you, Gentlemen that I address myself; I well know your Energy and the Scope you can give it. Carriages of every description are provided, as far as the means of obtaining them could be exerted.

29

Gentlemen, it is a Moment when we must suffer Privations; but whether your Persons are conveyed in Carts or Wagons, your Votes in the Castle Yard at York are equally good and to be as highly valued as if they had been conveyed in a coach and six. The Freeholder has most merit who climbs over the greatest Difficulties, to give his Vote and Support his own Rights.

I have the honour to be, most respectfully,
Your obliged and faithful Servant.
MILTON

York—May 28th—1807.

STATE OF THE POLL
Eighth Day Thursday May 28th 1807

WILBERFORCE	776	Total	8975
LASCELLES	689		7989
MILTON	697		7706

It was possible for each village and town to observe the rise and fall in the candidates' chances of success. Mr W. S. Stanhope, who was an agent for Mr Lascelles, wrote this letter to his son John, who was a student at Oxford, on the second day of the election.

York, May 22nd 1807

'I have but a moment to tell you I am engaged in the severest contest that ever was known. On Wednesday the poll began and closed leaving Milton in a minority but yesterday he got near three hundred a Head by getting early possession of the Avenues to the Polling Booths. Today Wilberforce who was last is regaining his ground fast and I fully expect that Mr Lascelles will beat the young Lord Milton, but the Contest will be dreadful and the expense enormous. . . .

And so it was, for brawls and fights became more frequent as each side attempted to intimidate the other's supporters.

Lascelles finished the first day with a slight lead over the others, but on the third day Lord Milton overtook him and retained the lead on the fourth day. On the fifth

Lascelles regained the lead and retained it with a falling margin until the twelfth day. On the thirteenth, Lord Milton had a lead of 59 votes which increased to 160 on the fourteenth and on the fifteenth to 188. At this point Lascelles gave up the struggle and the poll was closed. The Sheriff declared Mr Wilberforce and Lord Milton as the elected members and when these results were announced, on Friday, June 5th, the Whig rejoicings were tremendous.

Of course victory celebrations followed upon the announcement of the result. This meant a procession through the principal streets of the city following the customary speeches by the candidates.

It was the custom to chair the victorious members and one of the newspapers gave this description of the scene: 'The Band greeted the arrival of Lord Milton at the entrance to his hotel with the melody "See the Conquering Hero Comes". Lord Milton girt on the knight's sword and mounted a very elegant chair beautifully ornamented with laurel and orange-coloured ribbons, silks, satins, etc.

'The procession proceeded three times round the Castle Yard and then paraded the streets of the City accompanied by bands playing popular Whig tunes, the bells of the Minster and other churches pealing forth, to the beating of drums and the firing of cannon. The procession wended its way amidst the cheers of the populace and the enlivening smiles of innumerable ladies who lined the windows in every street through which the procession passed, waving orange-coloured handkerchiefs and exhibiting one of the most enchanting scenes the imagination can paint.' There was a victory song composed to the tune of 'Haste to the Wedding' and sung

The victorious candidate may lose his seat

by the victorious Whigs through the streets of York.
Here is one verse:

> COME haste to the chairing, our hearts are delighted,
> The day is our own a fair conquest is gain'd:
> Had MILTON not come we should never been right,
> And in our own country must slaves have remain'd.
> > Then let us be joyous,
> > For what can annoy us
> The day is our own and our hearts we'll regale:
> > Come see
> > True English liberty,
> Gladness abounding all over the vale.

The victory parade was not always an orderly affair as
you will see if you look at the illustration. Here those who
are chairing the member are being attacked by the supporters of the defeated candidate, who are doing their
best to overturn the chair at the precise moment that the
procession reaches the bridge so as to precipitate its
occupant into the stream below and give him a thorough
ducking. When the procession reached the *George* a dis-
appointed Tory threw a brick which narrowly missed
Lord Milton's head, and the mob attempted in vain to
overturn the chair. At a critical moment a band of Whig
supporters arrived on the scene and after a struggle they
managed to drive away the Tories, but not before the
mob had succeeded in stripping the chair of all its
decorations. Lord Milton then drove on in triumph to his
election banquet at Ettridges. In all probability it would
conclude very much like the one in the illustration. If you
look at this carefully you will discover many amusing
incidents. Can you see the brick that has been thrown
through the window at the agent and stunned him? Have
you noticed the man who is busy in making an attempt

33

The election banquet

to set fire to a friend's wig, or the man who is trying to
balance a glass of beer on the lady's hat? Look carefully
and see what else you can find for yourself. One party of
voters went to an inn eight miles from York to celebrate
the victory and left a bill of £2,300 for Lord Milton to
pay. Another party went to the *Skip Bridge Inn* and
celebrated well on £1,389 of wine, £195 of ale, £143 of
meat and ham, £36 of tea, coffee and tobacco, £199 of
hay and £23 of butter. Lord Milton had to pay this bill as
well.

Some months later the agent of Lord Milton went
round the various Wapentakes to pay the election
expenses of the freeholders who had voted for the success-
ful candidate. To claim payment each voter had to produce the certificate (which you read earlier) stating that
they had voted for Lord Milton. Here is a typical notice.

34

LORD MILTON'S ELECTION

THE FREEHOLDERS RESIDENT WITHIN THE WAPENTAKES OF
AGBRIGG AND MORLEY WHO VOTED FOR LORD MILTON AT THE
LATE ELECTION AND WISH TO BE REPAID THE EXPENSES INCURRED
BY THEM IN GOING TO, STAYING AT, AND RETURNING FROM
YORK.

are requested to apply to me
At any of the Times and Places mentioned viz.

BRADFORD

Thursday, Friday, and Saturday the 3rd, 4th, and 5th of December
next.

At Birstall on Monday, December 7th.

At Dewsbury on Tuesday and Wednesday the 8th and 9th.

WAKEFIELD

On Thursday and Friday the 10th and 11th.

By Order of His Lordship's Committee
Charles Bouns

York. November 28th 1807.

After all this, you will want to learn what happened to
the three candidates after the election was over. Wilberforce sat as a member until 1812 when he retired to Lord
Calthorpe's pocket borough of Bramber. Lord Milton
remained as one member until 1826 and after that year he
did not fight another election for he succeeded his father
as the fifth Earl Fitzwilliam in 1833. Mr Lascelles retired
in some annoyance, mourning his expenses of £100,000,
to the Earl of Abingdon's pocket borough of Westbury,
Wiltshire, where there were only thirteen voters. This
seat had been vacated for him by his brother Edward,
who chose to sit for the family borough of Northallerton.
He returned to Yorkshire in 1812 and this time secured
his nomination to Pontefract, the most scandalous rotten
borough in Yorkshire. In 1818 he succeeded his brother
Edward at Northallerton and when his father died he
came into the title and his election troubles were at an
end.

When Mr Lascelles went to take his borough of West-bury, the *Leeds Mercury* printed the following, which goes to the rhyme of 'pat a cake, pat a cake'.

A NEW SONG
SHERIFF
Run away, run away, Minister's man.
L——S.
So I will Sheriff, as fast as I can.
So twist me, and turn me, and mark me as out,
And send me to Westbury the easiest route.

A DRY NURSE

You may be interested in finding out and comparing the cost of the election of 1807 with that of 1955. Wilberforce spent £28,200 and both his opponents paid out more than £100,000 each, making a total of over a quarter of a million pounds. If we divide this total by the number of votes cast we find that the votes of Wilberforce average £2 10s. each, and those of Mr Lascelles and Lord Milton £10 each. In 1955 the twenty Yorkshire county divisions polled 940,000 votes at a total cost to the candidate of £30,000, or roughly 7½d. per vote. From this you will see that the two candidates for the one seat spent seven times as much as the candidates for twenty seats did in 1955. If we make allowances for the changes in the value of money, they spent very much more than that. We must all agree that only a very rich man indeed could afford to stand as Knight of the Shire for the county of York, in those days. It was fortunate indeed for Yorkshire that one of the richest men in the county, Earl Fitzwilliam, was also one of the most progressive in supporting the movement towards reform in the electoral system.

The Pontefract Election 1812

We have seen what happened in a county election and now we will find out how a borough election worked. The little town of Pontefract or Pomfret, in Yorkshire had the right to return *two* members to Parliament, a right which it had possessed for three hundred years. You will probably have heard of this town before, for it is the place where Pomfret Cakes are manufactured, and also Richard II was put to death in the castle dungeons in 1399. The 16,000 voters of Yorkshire had the right to elect two members and the 623 voters of Pontefract had the same right. There were no fewer than 203 boroughs of this kind in the country, of which more than half were to be found in Wiltshire and the counties bordering on the sea coast from Norfolk to Gloucestershire. Both Wiltshire and Cornwall had as many voters as the eight northern counties. The right to exercise a vote in these boroughs varied considerably. In some cases almost every householder had a right to vote; in others as at Richmond in Yorkshire, only the tenants of a burgage house had the right to a vote. Very often the freemen of the city and the *corporation* were the electors.

Here in Pontefract all the members of the corporation, the freemen of the borough, whether they lived in the city or not, and all male householders who paid *church rates* and *poor rates* had the right to vote in elections. Now unlike the city of Chichester, where the candidate for

37

whom they voted was always chosen by the Duke of Richmond, who lived at Goodwood, and who owned the greater part of the city, the freemen of Pontefract were anxious to keep their borough from passing into the control of one family. So you will realize that there was always very keen competition between the leading county families for the control of the borough of Pontefract.

The election we are now going to consider is the one that took place in 1812 following the dissolution of Parliament. When the Mayor received the Sheriff's writ to proceed with an election, he sent out the Town Crier with his bell to announce the election. '*Oyez*, Oyez, Oyez—these are to give notice that the worshipful, the Mayor of this town having received the Sheriff's precept for the election of two citizens to serve for this town in the new Parliament, will proceed to such election on Wednesday the 13th of October next at 9 of the clock in the forenoon in the Market Place of this town. God save the King.'

On 25th September 1812, four ambitious candidates succeeded in obtaining nomination at the meeting held for this purpose. One was our old friend of the election of 1807—Mr Henry Lascelles—whose family already controlled two boroughs and desired to get control of Pontefract. His opponents attacked Mr Lascelles saying that he wanted Pontefract only as a means by which he could strengthen his position in Parliament and not out of respect to the town. The second candidate was Mr Robert Milnes, a wealthy lawyer, who lived at Monk Fryston Hall and he too wanted to get a controlling interest in the borough. Lord Pollington, the heir of Lord Mexborough, of Methley Hall, a member of the famous Saville family, hoped to get back into Parliament via Pontefract. The last candidate was Mr Edward Hodgson of Stapleton Hall, a country squire, who owned a large game preserve. Now try to remember this, for the game preserve played an important part in the election. Each candidate then selected his colour under which he would fight the election. Lascelles retained blue as his colour: Milnes decided to use yellow for his favours, Lord Pollington decided upon scarlet and Mr Hodgson selected green. It is important that you remember these different colours for both Mr Lascelles and Mr Milnes were attacked in a poem, which you will read later, not by name but by their colours.

So the election campaign moved into its stride. Large numbers of ballads and posters appeared either supporting or attacking the candidates, just as they had done in the election of 1807. One poster attacked Mr Lascelles as a purchaser of Pomfret Cakes, which does not really mean that he bought cakes but votes. Here is one of the verses from the poem which shows that he expected to get back the money spent on bribing voters.

'No friendship I expect to find among the selfish crew,
  They'll prey on me, I'll prey on them; a practice nothing new.
  Their votes secured they may in vain expect my further grace,
  For seven long years this paltry town shall never see my face.
  And still the burthen of this song is, gold my friend shall be
  I've bought the cakes—I'll sell the cakes—the cakes are nought to
    me.'

Shortly after this ballad appeared, two brothers, John and Richard Foster were discussing the situation and as you read their conversation you should notice that they never mention Parliamentary Reform, but only the danger to the freedom of the borough. John asked Richard what he thought about the election parties. Richard replied that the great man Lascelles was determined to be returned as member for Pontefract. He then continued: 'If he is, he will never give us the liberty of being asked for our votes again, because he has threatened to turn his tenants out if they do not vote for him.' 'But,' said John, 'I thought this was a free borough?' 'No,' answered Richard, 'for certain gentlemen have threatened their tradesmen they shall not do their work if they do not let them have one vote. I called to see one last night and found him in very low spirits. We poor people must let them see we are not afraid of them, now that we have four candidates. Whatever we do we must not let them get the borough into their hands. I must give one vote to my landlord and the other to some honest man.'

The result of this conversation was the printing of a *satire* which was disguised as a duet which Lascelles and Milnes are singing to each other.

RICH AGAINST POOR

Says L–SC–LL–S to M–LN–S
'We'll have our own wills
Because we are backed by great friends:
  And as for the Poor
  We'll ask them no more
When once we've accomplished our ends.

Says M–LN–S to L–SC–LL–S
'Ne'er mind the ragg'd vassals
They shan't have a will of their own
  We'll do as we please
  And come in with ease
Then fetter the whole of the town.'

You will also remember how the opponents of Mr Lascelles had attacked him in the election of 1807, as a supporter of the slave trade. Here in Pontefract the same line of attack appeared and voters were warned that it was African gold from the slave trade that would buy their votes, as you will notice in these verses.

> 'What a base coalition has lately ta'en place,
> Twist a driver of slaves and a man of no grace.
> The Yellow and Blue think they play a fair game,
> And to rob us of freedom—fair freedom they aim.
> But electors be true, teach Yellow and Blue,
> That Scarlet your color, its rights can defend.'

> 'Shall it ever be said that Pomfret is sold,
> Or that voters are purchased with African's gold?
> While cant and low cunning with H – – – – – – e unite
> All the hopes of our sons and their wishes to blight,
> The flag of our Polly in triumph shall wave,
> For he'll crush peculation and rescue the slave.'

Lord Pollington was attacked on the grounds that he was under the influence of his mother and would do as she said. Further he was a supporter of the use of barley and what for distilling into spirits although bread was scarce and corn prices high.

Mr Hodgson made good use of his game preserve to support his cause in the election, and his agent John Tute of the Red Lion Inn took every opportunity to influence voters by bribes of game. Indeed one newspaper article declared that Mr Hodgson had emptied his manor of game, his larder of delicacies and his cellar of wine in order to feed the poor while the other candidates were content to stuff the already over-fed Aldermen with rich foods. According to one poster the principal source of Mr Hodgson's bribery was a plentiful supply of rabbits.

We've Rabbits young and Rabbits old,
Rabbits hot and Rabbits cold,
Rabbits tender—Rabbits tough,
And yet of them have not enough.
More Rabbits will our spirits raise,
For them shall Hodgson have our praise.
And if Lord P–LL–NGT–N oppose
The Rabbit friends—he'll meet with foes.

Two of the town's freemen David Simpson and Peter Jenkinson were discussing the election and as you follow their conversation you will notice that it was not Parliamentary Reform but the high level of taxation and the high price of bread that was their chief concern. 'Good morning, David,' said Peter, 'I wish you joy. Having boiled your pot for six months you are now a freeman of this ancient borough.' 'Boiled my pot,' answered David, 'my tea kettle you mean. Although we have a pot and water enough, we have nothing to put in except some excellent RABBITS which neighbour Hodgson sends.' 'He will get my vote for the rabbits he sent when Margery was ill for we could not afford meat at 9d. a pound and meal at 7s. a stone.' 'I agree,' replied Peter, 'for if HE gets to Parliament he will rid us of the tax on leather which has nearly ruined me as a shoemaker and taken my AWL from me, and if it goes on we must learn like the Scots to go barefoot.'

'You know Peter, that Lascelles and Milnes voted to send the expedition to Walcheren to attack Antwerp and we lost 2,000 good soldiers, without any word about making peace or reducing the price of corn. They received their reward for this, for Mr Lascelles' father has been made an Earl and Mr Milnes' brother has been given an easy government post at £5,000 a year. Let us

42

then both agree to vote for Hodgson. Besides, Milnes is a rascally lawyer, Lascelles looks like the Knave of Spades and Pollington is bribing people with dirty notes, so the only honest man is Hodgson.'

Now have you noticed two things in this conversation? The first is the use of the word AWL to mean two different things, for Peter Jenkinson was referring to it not only as a tool of his trade but also to his livelihood (all). The second is the reference to the war against Napoleon. In 1809 an attempt was made to invade Europe and a force was landed near Antwerp. The whole expedition was a disastrous failure and it is this that Peter and David were discussing.

Hodgson himself was attacked in turn for he was accused of having ambitions to create a borough interest out of his estate. His new building programme to erect sixty cottages was thought to be a plan to sell these along with Stapleton Hall, after the election, to anyone who wanted to be a candidate for the borough. In any case, they said, Hodgson's money-lending friends from London would sell up the estate to recover their costs in supporting Hodgson. Hence this notice.

TO BE SOLD BY AUCTION
(By Order of the Creditors)
ON WEDNESDAY NEXT AFTER THE ELECTION
ST–PL–T–N HALL
Together with its valuable and extensive RABBIT WARREN

Also the BOROUGH INTEREST belonging thereto
Conditions of sale with Mr William H–nt, Paradise Row, Pontefract, the solicitor to the Estate. Mr John T–te, the Warrener will show the premises.

How the election went you will see if you follow a conversation between two freemen, James Freeman and

43

Thomas Dobson. You will remember that an effort was to be made to prevent Pontefract from passing into the control of one family and becoming a closed borough.

'Well James, the election went briskly today and I wonder how it will end?'

'I don't know Thomas, but if Milnes and Lascelles are returned there will be no more elections and fine days like we have now, so elect new ones and we shall be certain of a contest the next time.'

'Haven't you heard James? Lascelles is to be returned for the county and so he cannot be member for both the county and Pontefract at the same time and that will mean another election.'

'Do I hear you correctly Thomas? That means if we return Lascelles we shall be able to have *TWO* elections instead of one?'

'Yes, James, so shake hands and vote for Lascelles and Hodgson.'

Mr Milnes and Mr Lascelles were declared as the two new members, but the borough had to hold another election on 22nd December to fill the place of Mr Lascelles who was returned for the county. This second election was even more scandalous than the one we have been considering. No wonder the chorus to a popular election song ran as follows:

'Come voters all let's join the throng nor leave the cause at random
Fill every buggy, whisky, dog cart, curricle or tandem.'

So Pontefract remained a free borough and these disgraceful elections went on unchecked until the Reform Bill of 1832 swept them away for ever.

The Fight for Reform

I think you will long ago have decided that these were shocking ways of running Parliamentary elections. There was nothing free about them and instead of getting the candidate elected whom the people wanted, the one with the most friends and money got in. You must be wondering why such ways were allowed to go on. Did no one think them wrong and try to reform Parliament?

The answer is that some people did, and in 1781 The Committee of Association for Parliamentary Reform in Yorkshire sent a petition to the Crown asking for better representation and an end to corruption and bribery. Unfortunately too many people were content to let things go on in the old way. Then, just as they were beginning to think about reform, an alarming event happened—the French Revolution. People heard that in France, noblemen's heads were rolling off under the *guillotine* and thousands were being executed. The English nobility and gentry were afraid that if they gave any more power to the people there might be a bloody revolution in England too. So they clamped down on any idea of giving the people more power in elections to Parliament.

The French Revolution ended in a great fight between the English and Napoleon which finished in 1815. With peace came a slump. British goods were not wanted abroad so unrest and unemployment began to grow. The men demobilized from the army and navy could not find jobs. Unemployed men and women began to collect in angry crowds and smash the new factory machines as, for instance, in Nottingham, because they thought it was throwing them out of work. Workers began to receive secret, anonymous letters, like this one calling a meeting at Bradford.

Call the distressed of Bradford, Idle, Wibsey, Windhill, Shipley, Horton, Bowling, Frizinghall and others to meet at the bottom of Bradford More on 26th March at 10 a.m. to consider if we must arise and fight or be pined to death and I wish we could put a stop to Worsit Millers, Merchant Manufactories, Comon Slibbing Billies and Wool Staplers. I expect there will be 20,000 and upwards. Let them know in Leeds and all the Towns adjacent. Keep the original. Let any Body have a Coppey. Your Suffering Brother and Loving Friend. 1816.

Have you noticed the curious spelling of several words in this letter?

There was an election at Westminster in 1818 which made many people realize how badly reform was needed. William Lamb, later Lord Melbourne, had been elected member, although he had been opposed by two other candidates. His supporters planned to chair the member through the streets and a crowd of some hundred bruisers and blackguards was collected who, with an escort of sixty Whig horsemen, were to have accompanied the procession through the streets to Burlington House. What actually happened was described in a letter by Lord Palmerston. Here is part of it for you to read.

Stanhope Street
London, March 2nd 1819.
'Crib, Gully and Caleb Baldwin declared that to chair was impossible and that they and Lamb should all be murdered if it was attempted.

46

On this the Committee gave it up and sent to stop the cavalry. The messenger missed them and at the appointed hour they arrived, found the avenues to Covent Garden blocked up by an immense crowd, cut their way through, found the chairing given up and had to cut their way back again. They were covered in mud and dirt, and some received some severe blows with the stones thrown at them. The mob chased them to Pall Mall and some even to Grosvenor Square. Lady Cowper (Lamb's sister) had a very narrow escape. She was returning from the Ladies' Committee at Amack's at this time. Her coachman happened to have Lamb's colours in his hat and in passing through St James Square to Pall Mall on her way to Melbourne House, the mob began pelting the carriage and one large stone nearly broke through the panel of the carriage about three inches below the side glass. Lady Caroline Lamb's carriage was also attacked in St James Street and a boy who was in it cut on the forehead by something thrown. These brutal outrages are quite peculiar to the present day. Lamb himself would have been torn to pieces but for the protection of a detachment of Life Guards.'

People began to agitate for Reform. Two of the leading men in this movement were William Cobbett and Henry Hunt. Cobbett was born in Farnham and served for a time in the army; after his discharge he published a reform paper, the *Weekly Register* and later described his travels through England in a book called *Rural Rides*. Hunt was born in Wiltshire and ran away from school to join the army; he was discharged for challenging the colonel of his regiment to a duel and became an eager reformer. Both these men said that if life was to be any better in England the first thing to do was to reform Parliament because in 1820 it did not represent the people of England. You will remember that great industrial changes were taking place at this time and the new towns were growing up with large numbers of inhabitants who had no representative in Parliament.

Henry Hunt and his friends, one of whom was Arthur

Thistlewood, began a violent agitation for reform. They thought that the best way of getting things done was to send a petition to the Prince Regent, later King George IV. With this idea in their minds these leaders advertised a meeting for this purpose which was to be held at Spa Fields, in London, on November 15th 1816. Posters were placed on walls and buildings which read like this:

'All distressed Tradesmen,
Manufacturers and Mariners
To Meet at Spa Fields on November 15th
to adopt Measures
with a view to their relief.'

As early as ten o'clock on the morning of the fifteenth the crowds began to collect and the account of the meeting which appeared on the following day in the *Morning Chronicle* estimated the number who attended the meeting as 20,000. At one o'clock Henry Hunt drove up in his coach and, standing on the roof, he addressed the crowd. Later he went into a neighbouring inn called *Merlin's Cave* and spoke to the crowd from an upstairs window. A resolution was passed to present a petition to Parliament asking for reform and then to meet at the same place on December 2nd to receive the reply.

Now in movements like this, there is always a small group who want things to move faster than they usually do. Arthur Thistlewood was the leader of this section and he pushed on with the plans. Posters were put out announcing the meeting for December 2nd and these were worded in such a way as to make people feel violent and want violent action. Here is the heading to one poster.

48

> 'FOUR MILLIONS IN DISTRESS
> Half a MILLION live in SPLENDID LUXURY.
> The NATION'S WRONGS must be REDRESSED.'

At the same time a pamphlet was printed with the title, *An Address to Suffering Britons* and this was smuggled into the prisons and from there a copy found its way to the Home Office. The pamphlet began like this:

> 'On Monday December 2nd the flag will be unfurled.
> Your liberty is planned and you will be restored to
> Your Country under a new Government.'

Can you see what Thistlewood and his friends planned to do? The operations were under the control of Thistlewood and four associates. They had managed to collect together a small quantity of explosives and pikes. Their intention was to attack the Bank of England, seize the Tower of London and open all the prisons.

On the appointed day the meeting was held, but before Hunt arrived some of the extreme leaders spoke and aroused a section of the crowd to fighting pitch. They moved off to break open a near-by gunsmith's shop from which they seized all the guns. This mob then divided into two sections, the first marching to the Royal Exchange and the second going to the Tower, intending to capture both places. However, the rebels' zeal cooled off as they marched along, so that the Lord Mayor of London, with a small band of special constables, managed to scatter the first group. When the second group arrived at the Tower and called on the soldiers to surrender, they were laughed at. The plotters were later arrested and imprisoned.

Parliament could not let these attempts at Reform by

violence go on; they had to be stamped out. So it suspended the *Habeas Corpus Act*, which meant that people could be imprisoned without trial for any length of time and it was also made illegal to hold meetings in order to clamour for reform. Of course all the reformers thought Parliament was wrong to stamp out these movements. A band of men set out from Manchester intending to march to London in protest. They carried blankets with them for their night's shelter and so they were known as the Blanketeers. However, the leaders of the march were arrested the day before the march took place and by the time the remainder had reached Macclesfield, the whole movement had come to an end.

In 1817 a boom and a good harvest stopped the disturbances for a while, for when people have enough to eat they are usually not so discontented. In July 1819, however, a meeting of people from Birmingham, Leeds, and Manchester, called a Parliamentary Convention, was planned. When the Birmingham reformers were told that this meeting was illegal they dropped their plan. The Manchester men were not put off so easily, for they sent an invitation to Henry Hunt to address a meeting on August 16th which was to be held in an open space called *St Peter's Fields*. Large numbers of men spent some time at drill in order that they might march to the meeting in an orderly fashion. Their opponents said that all this drill was a disguise for the armed rebellion that they were plotting. On August 16th some 50,000–60,000 people assembled in an orderly manner carrying banners. The magistrates, who had brought in special constables as well as detachments of the Lancashire and Cheshire Yeomanry, lost their nerve at the sight of this crowd and ordered the soldiers to arrest Hunt.

Samuel Bamford of Heywood, Lancashire, was present at this meeting and he described what took place:

'We had nearly got to the outside of the crowd when a noise and strange murmur arose toward the Church. Some persons said it was the Blackburn contingent coming; and I stood on tip-toe and looked in the direction whence the noise proceeded, and saw a party of cavalry in blue and white uniform, come trotting sword in hand round the corner of a garden wall and to the front of a new row of houses where they reined up. . . .'

The crowd greeted the arrival of the cavalry with loud cheers, but the cavalry drew their swords and spurred their horses into the crowd. Here let Samuel Bamford write:

'There was a general cry of "Stand Fast, they are riding upon us". The cavalry were in confusion; they evidently could not with all the weight of man and horse, penetrate that compact mass of human beings; and their swords were used to hew a way through the naked held-up hands and defenceless heads. There was a general cry of "Break Break". For a moment the crowd held back as in a pause; then there was a rush, heavy and resistless as a headlong sea and curses from those of the crowd who could not escape. When the crowd broke the yeomanry wheeled; and dashing wherever there was an opening, they followed pressing and wounding.'

Within ten minutes of the cavalry charge the field was an open and deserted place once more. A few persons were to be seen looking out from one of the new houses, others were assisting the wounded or carrying off the dead. The hustings remained, with a few broken flag-staves and a torn and gashed banner or two drooping from them, while scattered over the field were caps, bonnets, hats, shawls and shoes all trampled and bloodstained. The cavalry had dismounted and were quietly wiping their swords.

Later this terrible happening was called the Peterloo Massacre. Can you see why they invented the word

The cavalry charge into the crowd at Peterloo

Peterloo? This massacre made Arthur Thistlewood so angry that he only had one word after this—revenge. He returned to London and organized a new reform group. The plan made by Thistlewood and his friends was to murder the cabinet while they were at dinner with

Lord Harrowby. Having murdered the ministers of the Crown, they intended to seize Coutts and Childs Bank in order to get hold of some money, to set fire to several houses and then collect a mob to break into the gunsmiths' shops and take possession of all the arms in stock. They were to attack and take over the Bank of England as well as the Mansion House and murder all persons who attempted to leave London.

Their secret headquarters was in the attic of a house in Cato Street, just off the Edgware Road, in London. But they were betrayed, and on February 23rd 1820 the conspirators were surprised just as they were arming themselves for the attack. One member—a butcher—had arrived with a sack in which he hoped to carry away the heads of the murdered ministers, but the plotters were all arrested and tried at the Old Bailey. Five were condemned to transportation for life, five were sentenced to death and another group was discharged for lack of evidence. Thistlewood and his companions were executed on May 1st 1820, outside Newgate Prison. Large crowds came to witness the execution and so great were the numbers standing on the railings of St Sepulchre's Church that they collapsed and injured many spectators. Princess de Lieven, wife of the Russian Ambassador, who watched the execution, wrote this in a letter to a friend.

> 'The conspirators were hanged an hour ago and at the moment the streets are full of music and drums and of people wearing masks. It is the festival of chimney sweeps and they are dancing at every corner. It makes me sad.'

In 1882, a proposal to transfer one hundred seats, from the boroughs to the counties, was rejected, but Yorkshire obtained two additional members from the abolition of the borough of Grampound in Cornwall.

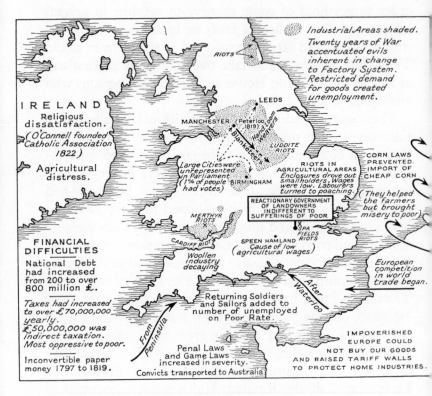

Industrial Areas shaded.
Twenty years of War accentuated evils inherent in change to Factory System. Restricted demand for goods created unemployment.

RIOTS

IRELAND
Religious dissatisfaction.
(O'Connell founded Catholic Association 1822)

Agricultural distress.

LEEDS

MANCHESTER Peterloo (1819) Hand loom Weavers

Blanketeers

LUDDITE RIOTS

Large Cities were unrepresented in Parliament. (1% of people had votes) BIRMINGHAM

RIOTS IN AGRICULTURAL AREAS
Enclosures drove out smallholders. Wages were low. Labourers turned to poaching.

CORN LAWS PREVENTED IMPORT OF CHEAP CORN

(They helped the farmers but brought misery to poor)

REACTIONARY GOVERNMENT OF LANDOWNERS INDIFFERENT TO SUFFERINGS OF POOR

MERTHYR RIOTS

CARDIFF RIOT

SPA FIELDS RIOTS

SPEEN HAMLAND
Cause of low (agricultural wages)

FINANCIAL DIFFICULTIES
National Debt had increased from 200 to over 800 million £.

Woollen industry decaying

European competition in world trade began.

Taxes had increased to over £70,000,000 yearly. £50,000,000 was indirect taxation. Most oppressive to poor.

Inconvertible paper money 1797 to 1819.

From Peninsula

After Waterloo

Returning Soldiers and Sailors added to number of unemployed on Poor Rate.

Penal Laws and Game Laws increased in severity.
Convicts transported to Australia

IMPOVERISHED EUROPE COULD NOT BUY OUR GOODS AND RAISED TARIFF WALLS TO PROTECT HOME INDUSTRIES.

The causes of distress after 1815

Reform Movements in a Yorkshire Town

Have you noticed that the first reform movement was led by a few energetic men and that the masses of the people only joined in when times were hard and unemployment high? They wanted BREAD more than VOTES and did not see quickly enough that the way to get the one was to demand the other. But in the large new towns which had no M.P.s of their own, business men began to see that if they wanted to get laws which favoured them, instead of always favouring the landowners and farmers, they must first get more power in Parliament. Gradually, also, the workers in the new factories and mills came to realize that the reform of Parliament would help them. Let us see how people began to work for this in Leeds, a big, growing town which was the centre of the woollen trade and still had no M.P.s of its own.

In 1826 there was an election. Because they had no candidates of their own to vote for, the business men of Leeds worked for the Yorkshire county election. Yorkshire had now got two extra members which had been taken away from rotten boroughs, so there were four M.P.s to be elected. Two of the candidates were our old friend Lord Milton and a wealthy flax-spinner from Leeds, John Marshall, who owned a lot of mills. Now it was a good thing to get a business man like this interested in politics but the trouble was that he was too rich. He would probably work in Parliament to get the Corn

Laws abolished, because this meant cheaper bread and he could pay low wages. But he did not really care about his workers at all and when he made friends with Lord Milton people in Leeds felt these two were not going to help them at all. They certainly wanted to get rid of the Corn Laws, but they had other troubles as well: the small clothiers were afraid that the new big power looms would ruin them and they would all become labourers; the workers felt bitterly about the way they and especially their poor children had to slave in the mills.

One of the best ways to get your opinions heard is to put them into print. Here is a poem which was published in a Leeds newspaper. The writer pretends that Milton and Marshall are singing a duet together, but can you see how bitter the song is about the poor workers? We call this a satire.

MILTON AND MARSHALL—A Duett

Now Corn shall be low
And trade shall be free
But still all shall bow
To thee and to me.

For Wages shall fall
And no one shall thrive
But Milton and Marshall
The drones of the hive

Now here is a notice which one of the small clothiers had printed and stuck round the town:

MACHINERY

Brother Clothiers—Would you have the evils of Machinery carried to their extremity, then vote for MARSHALL. He is the Man of Power Looms and Big Bens. He is the enemy of Hand Labour. Many of the wisest Statesmen think that Machinery may be carried too far—Mr Marshall, however, the Mill Owner of Holbeck, will encourage Machinery as far as possible.

If we small Manufacturers wish to become Labourers instead of MASTERS we must vote for Marshall and Power Looms.

A CLOTHIER

One of the election pamphlets attacked the wicked way in which small children were employed for very long hours in the mills. It was called The House That Jack Built and had a picture of John Marshall's mill—like this:

'Humbly dedicated to Mr John Marshall, Flax Spinner, Holbeck.
This is the House that Jack built.
This is the Flax, all heckled and torn, that lay in the House that Jack built.
These are the Children, all forlorn, who toil and slave from night till morn in spinning the Flax all heckled and torn, that lays in the House that Jack built.
This is the man, all shaven and shorn, for whom the poor children all forlorn toil and slave from night till morn, in spinning the Flax all heckled and torn, that lays in the House that Jack built.
This is John Bull, a Freeman born, whom the Man with his head all shaven and shorn, thinks to lead by the nose, while talking of corn while the poor Children, all forlorn, get so little for toiling from night till morn, in spinning his Flax all heckled and torn, that lays in the House that Jack built.

This is the LORD so very high born, who treated his LONGWOOL friends with scorn, yet has joined with the man all shaven and shorn, to lead John Bull by the nose, by talking of Corn, but if they don't mind they'll be tossed and torn, or be sent with the Children all forlorn, to twist from the Flax all heckled and torn, a Rope for to hang themselve some morn, in front of THE HOUSE THAT JACK BUILT.

The Lord in this is our old friend Lord Milton and of course you can see who Jack is. The Long Wool friends are the clothiers who had voted for Lord Milton against Lascelles in 1807. Now they know better and are against Milton and Marshall. They used all the arguments they could, even saying that Marshall's mills were the Orange Plantation of white slaves (orange was his colour) who were worse off than negro slaves in the Barbados.

All the same, Milton and Marshall got elected for the county (with two others). This made the people of Leeds see still more clearly that they must get votes for themselves and their own M.P.s. They must fight for Parliamentary reform first and get the other reforms afterwards. The way to fight for a reform is to band together in a group. Already in Leeds a few people had formed a Union for Parliamentary Reform and by 1829 they had managed to stir up a great many more to clamour for votes. The next step was to hold big meetings.

First the Radicals got going. They were the people who wanted the biggest reforms and on Monday, September 14th 1829, they held a reform meeting opposite the *Free Market Tavern*. The speaker was a Mr James Mann who was a bookseller in the market. 'England,' he said, 'had once been a happy and prosperous country, but now an immense number of its people were starving. This was because of the unfair way in which members were elected to Parliament. What England needed most was reform.'

The Radicals wanted a lot, but on March 18th, 1830, a much more cautious public meeting was held, led by the business men. The workers joined in, however, in such a quiet, orderly way that one of the chief newspapers, the *Leeds Mercury*, wrote: The meeting was conducted with utmost propriety and good temper, notwithstanding the distress under which some of the working classes are labouring. Even John Marshall, the M.P., had by now joined the moderate reformers. He spoke in favour of sending a petition to King George IV asking for some reform of Parliament. This was too cautious for the Radicals who wanted to ask definitely for secret ballots at elections and also that Parliament should not go on for more than three years without a general election. However, they did not get their way and the moderate petition, with 13,800 signatures was sent to London on April 3rd.

A third meeting was held on May 31st on Hunslet Moor. A petition signed by 132 persons was sent to the Mayor asking him to summon a public meeting to demand reform in the House of Commons. The Mayor refused to do so, partly because he was a Tory and not so interested in Reform, but the arrangements to hold the meeting went along. A band was hired from the neighbouring town of Morley to lead the procession from the city. Three banners appeared in the procession, one of which had a harp, shamrock, rose and thistle printed on it and underneath the words, 'UNIVERSAL AND RELIGIOUS LIBERTY.' The second had the words, 'HOLD TO THE LAWS'; while the third had a long inscription arranged like this:

'EXCESSIVE TAXATION GENERATES POVERTY
POVERTY GENERATES CRIME.
AN HOUR OF VIRTUOUS LIBERTY IS WORTH
AN ETERNITY OF BONDAGE.

59

Resolutions were put at the meeting that the distress in the country came from unnecessary wars and bad conduct of public affairs, so that reform was the only answer. The liberty the banners asked for was, in the first place, liberty to vote in Parliamentary elections.

King George IV died on June 16th 1830, and at once Parliament was dissolved and writs issued for a general election. In Yorkshire both Lord Milton and John Marshall refused to stand again as candidates, so Henry Brougham was put forward and adopted on June 23rd, together with Lord Morpeth.

On Tuesday, July 27th, Brougham visited Leeds and made an election speech to a crowd of 10,000 people after he had breakfasted in the Exchange Coffee Rooms. In his speech he said:

'We don't now live in the days of Barons—we live in the days of Leeds, of Bradford, of Halifax, of Huddersfield. We live in the days when men are industrious and desire to be free. I am for extending the rights of voting in the great towns of England. I go a great deal further. I am for extending the right of voting to that class of people who have no right now in any town of England—inhabitant householders—and I am for shortening the duration of Parliament.'

So Brougham wished to end the system by which the right to vote belonged only to those people who owned a piece of freehold land or house and extend the right to every person who lived in a house and paid rates.

The election took place in the Castle Yard, York, and afterwards a great victory dinner was held in Leeds to celebrate the return of Lord Morpeth and Henry Brougham as members for Yorkshire. Brougham spoke of his plan to fight for towns such as Leeds to send their own members:

'I find that Leeds, abounding with people, filled with wealth having vast and complicated interests which make it most of all probable that it should want the care and attention of its own representatives in Parliament, it is nevertheless utterly without these representatives as if it were some paltry rotten borough with half a dozen houses, with neither people nor wealth nor industry nor business to represent.'

So off they went to London to sit in Parliament under the Prime Minister, Earl Grey, who intended to introduce a bill to reform Parliament

Up and down
Wellington and Grey

The Reform Bill

You must imagine many other constituencies also electing M.P.s who were determined to reform Parliament.
These were the Whigs. But others, of course, were
equally determined to oppose it. These were the Tories.
The leader of the Tories in the House of Lords was the
Duke of Wellington and he said he thought the system of
electing members of Parliament was perfect! So everyone
was prepared for a big fight in Parliament between
Whigs and Tories.

Lord Grey introduced the first reform bill into the
House of Commons on March 1st 1831. The bill proposed that 60 of the old boroughs should lose their 119
seats in the House; that 60 more should have their members reduced to one seat each; that 7 new large towns
should each send two members, a further 20 new towns
should have one member each, and the 26 counties should
double their membership. The people who were to have
the vote were the 40s. freeholders, plus the £10 householders. The bill passed by one vote but it was defeated in
committee, so Earl Grey went to the King (William IV)
and asked him to dissolve Parliament, which he did.

This meant another general election immediately. In
Yorkshire four Whig candidates were nominated. The
Tories met at the offices of the *Leeds Intelligencer* to try
and nominate two candidates but they failed to do so.
This paper wrote:

'Well may the Advocates of the Bill exult. The Tories of Leeds, Barnsley, Bradford, etc., have done their duty . . . but we cannot say as much for the aristocracy and principal Tory landowners of the County.'

The gloom of this announcement should be compared with that of the *Leeds Mercury* (the Whig paper):

'Amidst the Orange colours which flame over Yorkshire not a scrap of rag of blue is anywhere to be seen except in a "No Dictation" placard, here and there, well bespattered with mud, and the blue flag of "forlorn hope" drooping in melancholy mockery from a window of the *Leeds Intelligencer* office.'

The four Whig candidates were elected amid scenes of wild rejoicing over a great victory for Reform. A procession of 30,000 people marched through the streets of Leeds on May 5th and on the following day a procession of freeholders, sporting orange colours, went to celebrate the victory at York. The *Leeds Mercury* published this comment on the results of the general election, on May 14th 1831. 'The great boroughmongers who have lorded it for so many years over the country and the government are defeated. The Lowthers are beaten in Cumberland. The Manners are expelled from Leicestershire; the Somersets are beaten in Gloucestershire; the Duke of Newcastle has been worsted at Newark; the Marquis of Exeter at Stamford; the Duke of Buckingham at Aylesbury. The Harewoods, Londonderrys, Bankes, Aclands, Tyrells, etc., etc., are losing the influence they have held for ages.'

Once again the reforming M.P.s trooped up to London and on September 21st Lord John Russell introduced a second Reform Bill into the Commons. This time it got a much bigger vote and passed its third reading in the Commons by a majority of one hundred. But of course most of the Lords voted against it and on October 8th it was rejected by a majority of forty-one, all the bishops voting against it. Can you think out why the Lords did not want to reform Parliament? When the news of this defeat came out many people were angry. Two London newspapers appeared with black borders for mourning and in Birmingham the church bells rang muffled peals, as if for a funeral. There were riots in Nottingham and Derby, but the worst trouble of all was in Bristol where people got put in prison for rioting. Sir Charles Wetherell, the attorney general under the Duke of Wellington, had opposed the first and second reform bills. On October 29th he came to Bristol to conduct the trials of

The city of Bristol goes up in flames

the prisoners in the city gaol. Although he had three troops of horse to guard him, the mob was so angry that the soldiers could not control it. They attacked and burned the Mansion House and marched to the old and new prisons where, after releasing the prisoners, they set the buildings on fire. Because the Bishop of Bristol had been one of those who had voted against the Reform Bill, they attacked and destroyed his palace. The gaol, toll house, bishop's palace, the Mansion House, the Customs and Excise office as well as two sides of Queen's Square, were all on fire. The damage was estimated at £100,000 or in today's currency at one million pounds. Though the cavalry finally restored order there was a danger of violent revolution.

In Leeds there was no violence because there was no property which belonged to any of the anti-reform Lords. A meeting was held on the September 26th to protest against the power of the Lords. One of the speakers said:

'Was there a man in the kingdom who could believe that a vote of the Cumberlands, the Newcastles, the Exeters, the Kenyons and the Carnarvons could induce people to put Gatton or Old Sarum upon a new trial? Or could it be supposed that it would or could perpetuate the system under which Leeds, Halifax, Huddersfield, Bradford, Manchester and Birmingham were excluded from all share in the privileges of the Constitution.'

All the names are the names of leading noblemen while Gatton and Old Sarum were the worst of the rotten boroughs. Can you think out for yourself what he meant by saying that Leeds and the other towns were excluded from all share in the privileges of the Constitution?

A crowd paraded the streets of Leeds with a stuffed

65

The Duke of Wellington

figure of the Duke of Wellington which they burnt like Guy Fawkes. They booed and cheered outside the office of the *Leeds Intelligencer* (the Tory newspaper) and let off fireworks. Francis Fawkes of Farnley Hall made plans to get the factory workers, miners and farm labourers to strike in protest. In London the mob threw stones through the windows of the Duke of Wellington's house and he had to post guards outside to prevent them getting in.

It was, as you see, chiefly the Lords, led by the Duke of Wellington, who were keeping the Reform Bill from passing. But have you noticed that one nobleman was the leader of the reforming party—Lord Grey? There were others with him, too, and as the Lords began to realize how angry people were getting, more began to think it would be better to vote for the bill than have a bloody revolution and find themselves being hung from the lamp-posts. The new king, William, also realized that the people were determined to get the bill passed, so he tried to persuade the bishops to vote for it next time it came up to the House of Lords. But too many of the Lords were still pig-headed, so Lord Grey asked the King if he would be willing to make a whole lot of new lords, so that the die-hards could be out-voted and the bill got through. He agreed to make twelve new ones at first, as a threat to the obstinate lords that if they would not vote for the bill he would create more lords.

So the Third Reform Bill, which had already passed the Commons, went to the Lords and in April 1832 got through its second reading. But then the Lords postponed their final vote and the Commons began to get angry and impatient. Lord Grey asked the King to make fifty new lords, but this time the King was nervous of making so many at once and refused. So Lord Grey resigned as prime minister and all his ministers with him.

When this news reached the provinces, the *Leeds Mercury* came out with the following comment.

'A great Calamity has befallen England.
The Boroughmongers have triumphed.
The Reform Bill has been strangled.
The King has Refused to make Peers and
The Grey and Brougham administration has Resigned.'

There were demonstrations in York against those who had caused the resignation of Lord Grey. The *Leeds Mercury* reported that:

'On Wednesday Evening about nine of the clock, 2,000 persons collected together in York and paraded the city with an effigy of the Archbishop: they proceeded to Bishopthorpe when, after a noisy demonstration, they burned it in front of the palace. The clock at the entrance was damaged and a few windows were broken. The crowd dispersed when the news that the military were approaching reached them. On Thursday evening a crowd collected about ten o'clock and they burned an effigy of Captain Price, the leader of the Tories in York. The crowd broke his windows and destroyed his garden fence.'

Now the King hoped to persuade the Duke of Wellington to become prime minister and get a very moderate reform bill passed. But the Commons, with all the people in the country behind them, were now very angry and

67

determined to have Lord Grey back and get a full and proper reform bill. While the Duke of Wellington was hesitating, people all over the country held meetings and sent up petitions clamouring for proper reform. One man who worked very hard for this was Francis Place, a tailor who lived in Charing Cross. As he sat in his small room thinking what he could do to help on reform, he had the good idea of putting up posters on which he printed TO STOP THE DUKE, GO FOR GOLD! You see, if a great many people took their money out of the banks, this would upset trade and prevent the government from carrying on. Some of the newspapers printed cartoons about reform. Look at the one on the opposite page. Can you see that the tree which the reformers are trying to cut down is called the Rotten Borough System, and that the old gentleman with white hair who is trying to hold up the tree is the Duke of Wellington? Each of the nests represents a famous rotten borough. The man and woman who are standing on the hill in the left-hand corner at King William IV and his Queen.

As a result of all these efforts, Wellington was persuaded not to take on the government. So Grey returned as prime minister. Now at last the Third Reform Bill came up for its third reading in the House of Lords. In order to let it go through a number of the Lords promised not to go and vote against it, but the way they made these promises made people suspicious that they would not keep them. So Lord Grey insisted that the King should solemnly promise to create as many new lords as should be needed to pass the Reform Bill and make it law. This finally frightened the Lords into voting for it and on June 4th the bill got through its third and last reading! Then the Third Reform Bill received the royal assent and

The attack on the rotten boroughs

became an Act of Parliament—part of the law. All over the country people rejoiced, ringing church bells, holding feasts and letting off fireworks.

The *Leeds Mercury* had several reports of the Reform Bill celebrations in Yorkshire. At a victory dinner at Oulton, near Leeds the following song was sung:

> It was on the twenty-third of May
> Year eighteen thirty-two.
> We did the orange flag display
> Above the haughty blue.

With hearts united as one man
Fearless of foe or storm,
To Wakefield, Yorkshire men did go
For Grey and his Reform

Chorus

With Bentley we did go boys,
With Bower we did go,
To save the Crown at Wakefield Town
The Blues to overthrow.

'At Otley on Tuesday evening a grand ball was given. On Wednesday the old women and ladies had a tea drinking in honour of the Reform Bill. At Thornton, near Bradford, on Tuesday, the females of Messrs Wright and Sons manufactory were treated to a public breakfast.'

'Pudsey (Leeds). The Masters of seven woollen manufactories regaled the whole of their men and boys with roast beef, plum pudding and strong ale. Afterwards they walked in procession together, with the females, to church where an appropriate sermon was preached by Revd. D. Jenkins.'

These are a selection from the large number of reports in the paper for June 16th and 23rd.

This Act did not do as much as the Radicals would have liked. It did not give everyone the vote and it did not make the ballot secret. There were plenty more reforms of Parliament for which people had to go on working. But it was the first big reform of Parliament to take place in England and the first step is always the hardest. Find out, if you can, about the reforms which have taken place since then.

You may have thought that the only way to get any reform was to have a violent revolution like the French. But now you have seen that the people of England, by working hard and pushing hard in all sorts of ways, were able to force through the reform of Parliament without cutting off anyone's head or hanging the Lords from lamp-posts. Have you noticed the different ways in which they 'pushed'—by holding public meetings and marching in processions with banners, by sending up resolutions and petitions to the King or to Parliament, by printing pamphlets and songs and cartoons in newspapers? These are some of the ways in which people in the past have worked for great reforms. If you go on and find out about other great reforms which followed this first big step in the nineteenth century, you will discover that reforms in town government, in the factories and coal-mines, in the poor law and so on, were all carried through without any violence or shedding of blood. But the reformers had to work very hard to convince others that unjust and evil things must be altered. We still have to fight against injustice and cruelty, and the best way to do this is still to try and persuade people that wrong things must be righted.

SOME CLAUSES OF THE 1832 REFORM ACT

Only some sections of the Reform Act (2. William IV, c. 45) are quoted below.

1. It is enacted that each of the Boroughs enumerated . . . that is to say, Old Sarum, Newton, St Michael's, Gatton, Bamber, Bossiney, Dunwich, Ludgershall, Beeralston, West Looe, St German's, Newport, Aldborough, Camelford, Hindon, East Looe, Corfe Castle, Great Bedwin, Yarmouth, Queenborough, Castle Rising, East Grinstead, Higham Ferrars, Wendover, Weobley, Winchelsea, Tregony, Haslemere, Saltash, Orford, Callington, Newton, Ilchester, Boroughbridge, Stockbridge, New Romney, Hedon, Plympton, Seaford, Heylesbury, Steyning, Whitchurch, Wootton Bassett, Fowey, Milbourne Port, Minehead, Bishop's Castle, Okehampton, Appleby, Lostwithiel, Brackley and Amersham shall cease to return any Members to Parliament.

2. That each of these Boroughs, Petersfield, Ashburton, Eye, Westbury, Wareham, Midhurst, Woodstock, Wilton, Malmesbury, Liskeard, Reigate, Hythe, Lyme Regis, Droitwich, Launceston, Shaftesbury, Thirsk, Christchurch, Horsham, Great Gromsby, Calne, Arundel, St Ives, Rye, Clitheroe, Morpeth, Helston, Northallerton, Wallingford and Dartmouth shall return one Member only.

3. That each of the places named, Manchester, Birmingham, Leeds, Greenwich, Sheffield, Sunderland, Devonport, Wolverhampton, Finsbury, Marylebone, Lambeth, Bolton, Bradford, Blackburn, Oldham, Brighton, Halifax, Stockport, Stoke on Trent and Stroud shall return Two Members each to serve in Parliament.

4. That each of the places named, Ashton-under-Lyne, Bury, Chatham, Cheltenham, Dudley, Frome, Gateshead, Huddersfield, Kidderminster, Kendal, Rochdale, Salford, South Shields, Tynemouth, Wakefield, Walsall, Warrington, Whitby, Whitehaven and Merthyr Tydvil shall send One Member each to serve in Parliament.

5. The existing rights of Freeholders are to be maintained.

6. In every city or borough any owner or tenant of any house which has a yearly value of £10, shall if he is registered be able to vote for the said city or borough. No person shall be registered who has lived in that place for less than six months.

7. No person shall be registered as a voter who in the past twelve months has received alms or poor relief.

8. No person shall be registered as a voter in the county unless he is in the actual possession of rents or profits for six months before or an owner of land for not less than twelve months.

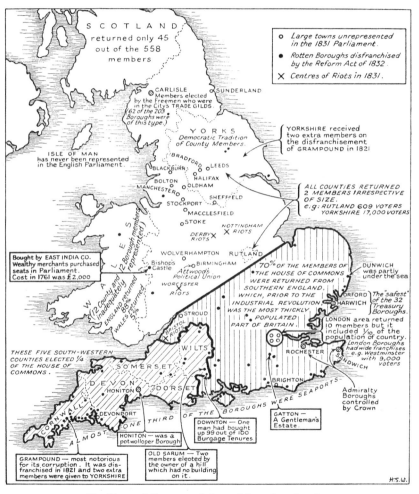

The Electoral System and the need for reform in 1832

THINGS TO DO

1. Write a diary kept by one of Lord Milton's supporters during the 1807 election, *or* write a letter from a Yorkshire freeholder who has been conveyed into York to vote for Mr Lascelles, telling his wife about the journey and the goings-on in York.

2. Draw an election cartoon for either the Yorkshire Election of 1807 or the Pontefract Election of 1812.

3. Draw or paint a picture of Lord Milton's triumphal procession round York as the Conquering Hero.

4. Write an election song to be sung to a popular modern tune.

5. Find out about a modern Parliamentary Election. How are the candidates nominated? What are the qualifications for voters?

Find out also as much as you can about the election of a President in the United States of America. What are the chief differences between these modern elections and those described in this book?

6. Find out which are your nearest cities and boroughs with the right to elect their own M.P.s and how many M.P.s your country has.

7. The great Reform Act of 1832 was only the beginning of Parliamentary reform. Find out what other great reforms of Parliament have been made since then.

8. Ask at the library for books which tell you more about some of the great reformers, e.g. William Wilberforce, Francis Place, Robert Owen, Lord Shaftesbury.

9. Hold an imaginary debate in Parliament (either in the House of Commons or Lords) on The 1832 Reform Bill.

10. Discuss:

    (a) Why could the House of Lords be frightened into passing the Third Reform Bill by the mere threat of the King creating a great many new Lords?

    (b) Does Parliament need reforming today?

    (c) Do people still organize great marches of protest?

    (d) If you wanted to bring about a reform today what methods would you use to make people listen to you?

GLOSSARY

to apprize : to tell

assessor : man who decides people's claims

ballad : popular song

ballot : a paper used to give a secret vote

ballot box : the steel box into which the voting papers are placed

barouche : four-wheeled carriage

bribe : a gift offered to a person to influence his conduct

burgage house : a town house which gave the owner or sometimes the tenant the right to vote

by-election : election in one place only, when the member dies or retires.

candidate : one who is proposed for election

to canvas : to ask people to vote for a certain person

check clerk : a person who checked and recorded votes at an election

church rate : tax to support the church

corporation : governing council in a city or borough

curricle : light, two-wheeled carriage with two horses

fly-wagon : a fast carriage

freeholder : a person who owns his own land

gig : light, two-wheeled carriage with one horse

guillotine : machine for chopping off people's heads

Habeas Corpus : 'You must have the body.' The first words of a Latin order addressed to the keeper of a prison telling him to bring a certain prisoner into court for trial

hustings : the platform from which candidates spoke to electors

land tax : a charge on land to meet public expenses

libel : a publication which says untrue things about a person

to nominate : to propose a candidate for election

Oyez : 'Listen!'—an old French word called out by the Town Crier to attract people's attention

pamphlet : printed leaflet

plantation : a large estate usually worked by slaves

Pocket Borough : a town returning a member to Parliament where the election is controlled by one family

polling booth : a temporary structure for voting in at elections

polling station : the centre at which voters register their votes

poor rate : tax to help the poor

precept : order

Register of Voters : a list of persons entitled to vote

Returning Officer : the presiding officer at elections

to scour : to clean

Sheriff : officer at the head of a county

show of hands : raising one's hand in either approval or disapproval

tenant : a person renting land or houses from a landlord

tithe : a tax of one tenth upon all produce which was levied by the Church

toleration : allowing people freedom, e.g. to worship as they choose, even when you disagree with them

unopposed : without any resistance offered

wapentake : a unit of administration of local government in the north